D1576063

To:

From:

The text in this book is excerpted from
The World According to Mister Rogers:
Important Things to Remember
by Fred Rogers,
originally published by Hyperion in 2003.
Copyright © 2003
by Family Communications, Inc.
All rights reserved.

Designed by Karine Syvertsen

Published in 2006
by arrangement with Hyperion.
Peter Pauper Press, Inc.
202 Mamaroneck Avenue
White Plains, NY 10601
All rights reserved
ISBN 978-1-59359-914-0
Printed in China
28 27

Visit us at www.peterpauper.com

WISDOM FROM

The World According
to
Mister Rogers

Important Things to Remember

CONTENTS

FOREWORD BY
Joanne Rogers

There were always quotes tucked away in Fred's wallet, next to his neatly folded bills, or in the pages of his daily planner book. Perhaps he liked having words of wisdom close to him, as if he wanted—or needed—to be constantly reminded of what was important in life. The outside world may have thought his qualities of wisdom and strength came naturally to him, but those close to him knew that he was constantly striving to be the best that he could be. He was as human as the rest of us.

The person Fred became in his later years came out of growth and struggle. As he got older, it seemed as if the nurturing of his soul and mind became more and more important. . . . If I were asked for three words to describe him, I think those words would be *courage, love*, and *discipline*—perhaps in that very order.

When I think of the entire *persona* of Fred Rogers, my inclination is to put him on a very high pedestal, despite the frailties that are part of being human. Oh, did I mention what a *kind* person he was? I suppose that is part of everyone's experience of Fred—even those who knew him for only a couple of minutes. I don't mean to sound boastful, but he was my icon before he was anyone else's. Being Mrs. Fred Rogers has been the most remarkable life I could ever have imagined.

The Courage to Be Yourself

Discovering the truth about ourselves is a lifetime's work, but it's worth the effort.

Some days, doing "the best we can" may still fall short of what we would like to be able to do, but life isn't perfect—on any front—and doing what we can with what we have is the most we should expect of ourselves or anyone else.

Confronting our feelings and giving them appropriate expression always takes strength, not weakness. . . . It takes strength to talk about our feelings and to reach out for help and comfort when we need it.

Who you are inside is what helps you make and do everything in life.

Whatever we choose to imagine can be as private as we want it to be. Nobody knows what you're thinking or feeling unless you share it.

How many times have you noticed that it's the little quiet moments in the midst of life that seem to give the rest extra-special meaning?

When my mother or my grandmother tried to keep me from climbing too high, my grandfather would say, "Let the kid walk on the wall. He's got to learn to do things for himself."
I loved my grandfather for trusting me so much.

It's not the honors and the prizes and the fancy outsides of life that ultimately nourish our souls. It's the knowing that we can be trusted, that we never have to fear the truth, that the bedrock of our very being is firm.

Solitude is different from loneliness, and it doesn't have to be a lonely kind of thing.

You rarely have time for everything you want in this life, so you need to make choices. And hopefully your choices can come from a deep sense of who you are.

All life events are formative. All contribute to what we become, year by year, as we go on growing. As my friend the poet Kenneth Koch once said, "You aren't just the age you are. You are all the ages you ever have been!"

I've often hesitated in beginning a project because I've thought, "It'll never turn out to be even remotely like the good idea I have as I start." I could just "feel" how good it could be. But I decided that, for the present, I would create the best way I know how and accept the ambiguities.

I believe it's a fact of life that what we have is less important than what we make out of what we have. The same holds true for families: It's not how many people there are in a family that counts, but rather the feelings among the people who are there.

When I was a boy I used to think that strong meant having big muscles, great physical power; but the longer I live, the more I realize that real strength has much more to do with what is not seen. Real strength has to do with helping others.

The thing I remember best about successful people I've met all through the years is their obvious delight in what they're doing . . . and it seems to have very little to do with worldly success. They just love what they're doing, and they love it in front of others.

Little by little we human beings are confronted with situations that give us more and more clues that we aren't perfect.

All our lives, we rework the things from our childhood, like feeling good about ourselves, managing our angry feelings, being able to say good-bye to people we love.

The child is
in me still . . .
and sometimes
not so still.

Understanding
Love

Understanding love is one of the hardest things in the world.

Deep within us—
no matter who we are—
there lives a feeling of
wanting to be lovable,
of wanting to be the kind of
person that others like to be
with. And the greatest thing
we can do is to let people
know that they are loved
and capable of loving.

Love isn't a state of perfect caring. It is an active noun like struggle. To love someone is to strive to accept that person exactly the way he or she is, right here and now.

Each generation, in its turn, is a link between all that has gone before and all that comes after. That is true genetically, and it is equally true in the transmission of identity. Our parents gave us what they were able to give, and we took what we could of it and made it part of ourselves.... We, in our turn, will offer what we can of ourselves to our children and their offspring.

It's the people
we love the most
who can make us
feel the gladdest . . .
and the maddest!
Love and anger are
such a puzzle!

If the day ever came when we were able to accept ourselves and our children exactly as we and they are, then, I believe, we would have come very close to an ultimate understanding of what "good" parenting means. It's part of being human to fall short of that total acceptance—and often far short. But one of the most important gifts a parent can give a child is the gift of accepting that child's uniqueness.

It always helps
to have people
we love beside us
when we have
to do difficult
things in life.

One of my
wise teachers,
Dr. William F. Orr,
told me, "There is
only one thing evil
cannot stand and
that is forgiveness."

*Love and trust,
in the space between
what's said and
what's heard in our
life, can make all
the difference in
this world.*

There's something
unique about being
a member of a family
that really needs you in
order to function well.
One of the deepest
longings a person can
have is to feel needed
and essential.

Actor David Carradine, son of John Carradine, said in gratitude of his father's accomplishments, "I could stand on his shoulders and feel twice as tall." That each generation could stand on the shoulders of the last and feel twice as tall is a poetic hope for all our families.

The gifts we treasure most over the years are often small and simple. In easy times and in tough times, what seems to matter most is the way we show those nearest us that we've been listening to their needs, to their joys, and to their challenges.

As parents, we need to try to find the security within ourselves to accept the fact that children and parents won't always like each other's actions . . . But we need to know, at the same time, that moments of conflict have nothing to do with whether parents and children really love one another. It's our continuing love for our children that makes us want them to become all they can be, capable of making sound choices.

Forgiveness is a strange thing. It can sometimes be easier to forgive our enemies than our friends. It can be hardest of all to forgive people we love. Like all of life's important coping skills, the ability to forgive and the capacity to let go of resentments most likely take root very early in our lives.

In times of stress,
the best thing we can
do for each other is
to listen with our ears
and our hearts
and to be assured that
our questions are
just as important
as our answers.

*One of the strongest things
we have to wrestle with in
our lives is the significance
of the longing for
perfection in ourselves and
in the people bound to
us by friendship or
parenthood or childhood.*

The greatest
gift you ever
give is your
honest self.

It's not always easy for
a father to understand the
interests and ways of
his son. It seems the songs of
our children may be in
keys we've never tried.
The melody of each
generation emerges from
all that's gone before. Each
one of us contributes in
some unique way to the
composition of life.

I believe that infants
and babies whose mothers
give them loving comfort
whenever and however they
can are truly the fortunate ones.
I think they're more likely to
find life's times of trouble
manageable, and I think
they may also turn out to be
the adults most able to pass
loving concern along
to the generations that
follow after them.

Learning and loving go hand in hand. My grandfather was one of those people who loved to live and loved to teach.... He'd help me find something wonderful in the smallest of things, and ever so carefully, he helped me understand the enormous worth of every human being.

In the external scheme of things, shining moments are as brief as the twinkling of an eye, yet such twinklings are what eternity is made of—moments when we human beings can say "I love you," "I'm proud of you," "I forgive you," "I'm grateful for you." That's what eternity is made of: invisible, imperishable *good stuff.*

We need to help people to discover the true meaning of love. Love is generally confused with dependence. Those of us who have grown in true love know that we can love only in proportion to our capacity for independence.

Love is like infinity: You can't have more or less infinity, and you can't compare two things to see if they're "equally infinite." Infinity just is, and that's the way I think love is, too.

*Human relationships are
primary in all of living.
When the gusty winds
blow and shake our lives,
if we know that people care
about us, we may bend
with the wind . . . but
we won't break.*

When we love a person, we accept him or her exactly as is: the lovely with the unlovely, the strong along with the fearful, the true mixed in with the façade, and of course, the only way we can do it is by accepting ourselves that way.

The Challenges
of Inner
Discipline

Imagining something may be the first step in making it happen, but it takes the real time and real efforts of real people to learn things, make things, turn thoughts into deeds or visions into inventions.

Discipline is a teaching-learning kind of relationship as the similarity of the word *disciple* suggests. By helping our children learn to be self-disciplined, we are also helping them learn how to become independent of us as, sooner or later, they must. And we are helping them learn how to be loving parents to children of their own.

How great it is when we come to know that times of disappointment can be followed by times of fulfillment; that sorrow can be followed by joy; that guilt over falling short of our ideals can be replaced by pride in doing all that we can; and that anger can be channeled into creative achievements . . . and into dreams that we can make come true!

I like to swim, but there are some days I just don't feel much like doing it—but *I do it anyway!* I know it's good for me and I promised myself I'd do it every day, and I like to keep my promises. That's one of my disciplines. And it's a good feeling after you've tried and done something well. Inside you think, "I've kept at this and I've really learned it—not by magic, but by my own work.

What makes the difference between wishing and realizing our wishes? Lots of things, and it may take months or years for a wish to come true, but it's far more likely to happen when you care so much about a wish that you'll do all you can to make it happen.

A young apprentice applied to a master carpenter for a job. The older man asked him, "Do you know your trade?" "Yes, sir!" the young man replied proudly. "Have you ever made a mistake?" the older man inquired. "No, sir!" the young man answered, feeling certain he would get the job. "Then there's no way I'm going to hire you," said the master carpenter, "because when you make one, you won't know how to fix it."

There is no normal life that is free of pain. It's the very wrestling with our problems that can be the impetus for our growth.

It came to me ever so slowly
that the best way to know the
truth was to begin trusting
what my inner truth was . . .
and trying to share it—
not right away—only after
I had worked hard at trying
to understand it.

The great poet Rainer Maria Rilke wrote: "Be patient towards all that is unsolved in your heart, and learn to love the questions themselves."

There's an old Italian proverb: Qui va piano, va sano, va lentano. That means: "The person who goes quietly, goes with health and goes far." Hurrying up and using a lot of shortcuts doesn't get us very far at all.

I wrote in a song that in
the long, long trip of growing,
there are stops along the way.
It's important to know when we
need to stop, reflect, and receive.
In our competitive world, that
might be called a waste of time.
I've learned that those times can
be the preamble to periods
of enormous growth.

What makes the difference between wishing and realizing our wishes? Lots of things, of course, but the main one, I think, is whether we link our wishes to our active work. It may take months or years, but it's far more likely to happen when we care so much that we'll work as hard as we can to make it happen. And when we're working toward the realization of our wishes, some of our greatest strengths come from the encouragement of people who care about us.

When we can resign ourselves to the wishes that will never come true, there can be enormous energies available within us for whatever we can do.

Feeling good about who we are doesn't come just from people telling us they like us. It comes from inside of us: knowing when we've done something helpful or when we've worked hard to learn something difficult or when we've "stopped" just when we were about to do something we shouldn't, or when we've been especially kind to someone else. Along with the times we're feeling good about who we are, we can experience times when we're feeling bad about who we are.

It's true that we take a great deal of our own upbringing on into our adult lives and our lives as parents; but it's true, too, that we can change some of the things that we would like to change. It can be hard, but it can be done.

As work grows out of play, an attitude toward work grows with it—an attitude that may persist all through our workaday life. That attitude can have a lot to do with how we accept challenges, how we can cope with failures, and whether we can find the inner fulfillment that makes working, in and of itself, worthwhile.

We Are
All
Neighbors

From the song
Won't You Be My Neighbor?

I have always wanted
to have a neighbor
Just like you!
I've always wanted to live in a
Neighborhood with you.
So let's make the most
of this beautiful day;
Since we're together
we might as well say,
Would you be mine?
Could you be mine?
Won't you be my neighbor?

It's no secret that I like to get to know people—and not just the outside stuff of their lives. I like to try to understand the meaning of who people are and what they're saying to me.

As human beings, our job in life is to help people realize how rare and valuable each one of us really is, that each of us has something that no one else has—or ever will have—something inside that is unique to all time. It's our job to encourage each other to discover that uniqueness and to provide ways of developing its expression.

When I was very young,
most of my childhood heroes
wore capes, flew through the
air, or picked up buildings
with one arm. They were
spectacular and got a lot of
attention. But as I grew, my
heroes changed, so that now
I can honestly say that anyone who does anything to
help a child is a hero to me.

*We want to raise
our children
so that they can take
a sense of pleasure
in both their own
heritage and the
diversity of others.*

When you combine your own intuition with a sensitivity to other people's feelings and moods, you may be close to the origins of valuable human attributes such as generosity, altruism, compassion, sympathy, and empathy.

Jane Addams, writing about her Twenty Years at Hull House, said, "People did not want to hear about simple things. They wanted to hear about great things—simply told."

Music has given me a way of expressing my feelings and my thoughts, and it has also given me a way of under-standing more about life. For example, as you play together in a symphony orchestra, you can appreciate that each musician has something fine to offer. Each one is different, though, and you each have a different "song to sing." When you sing together, you make one voice. That's true of all endeavors, not just musical ones. Finding ways to harmonize our uniqueness with the uniqueness of others can be the most fun—and the most rewarding—of all.

If you could only sense how important you are to the lives of those you meet; how important you can be to the people you may never even dream of. There is something of yourself that you leave at every meeting with another person.

Whether we're a pre-schooler or a young teen, a graduating college senior or a retired person, we human beings all want to know that we're acceptable, that our being alive somehow makes a difference in the lives of others.

The real issue in life is not how many blessings we have, but what we do with our blessings. Some people have many blessings and hoard them. Some have few and give everything away.

The purpose of life is to listen—to yourself, to your neighbor, to your world and to God and, when the time comes, to respond in as helpful a way as you can find . . . from within and without.

Please think of the children first. If you ever have anything to do with their entertainment, their food, their toys, their custody, their day or night care, their health care, their education—listen to the children, learn about them, learn from them. Think of the children first.

One of the greatest dignities of humankind is that each successive generation is invested in the welfare of each new generation.

More and more I've come to understand that *listening* is one of the most important things we can do for one another. Whether the other be an adult or a child, our engagement in listening to who that person is can often be our greatest gift. Whether that person is speaking or playing or dancing, building or singing or painting, if we care, we can listen.

Peace means far more than the opposite of war!

Beside my chair is a saying in French. It inspires me every day. It's a sentence from Saint-Exupéry's *The Little Prince*, and it reads, "*L'essential est invisible pour les yeux.*" (What is essential is invisible to the eyes.) The closer we get to know the truth of that sentence, the closer I feel we get to wisdom. That which has real value in life in any millennium is very simple. Very deep and very simple! It happens inside of us—

in the "essential invisible" part of us, and that is what allows everyone to be a potential neighbor.

The urge to make and build seems to be an almost universal human characteristic. It goes way beyond meeting our need for survival and seems to be the expression of some deep-rooted part of being human. . . . But we don't have to understand all of someone else's creative efforts. What's important is that we communicate our respect for their attempts to express what's inside themselves.

As different as we are from one another, as unique as each one of us is, we are much more the same than we are different. That may be the most essential message of all, as we help our children grow toward being caring, compassionate, and charitable adults.

Imagine what our real neighborhoods would be like if each of us offered, as a matter of course, just one kind word to another person. There have been so many stories about the lack of courtesy, the impatience of today's world, road rage and even restaurant rage. Sometimes, all it takes is one kind word to nourish another person. Think of the ripple effect that can be created when we nourish someone. One kind empathetic word has a wonderful way of turning into many.

When I was a boy and I would
see scary things in the news,
my mother would say to me,
"Look for the helpers. You will
always find people who are
helping." To this day, especially
in times of "disaster," I
remember my mother's words,
and I am always comforted
by realizing that there are still
so many helpers—so many
caring people in this world.

You don't ever have to do anything sensational for people to love you. When I say, "It's you I like," I'm talking about that part of you that knows that life is far more than anything you can *ever see or hear or touch* . . . that deep part of you that allows you to stand for those things without which humankind cannot survive: *love* that conquers hate, *peace* that rises triumphant over war, and *justice* that proves more powerful than greed.

So in all that you do in all of your life, I wish you the strength and the grace to make those choices which will allow you and your neighbor to become the best of whoever you are.

I consider that what I do through *Mister Rogers' Neighborhood* is my ministry. A ministry doesn't have to be only through a church, or even through an ordination. And I think we all can minister to others in this world by being compassionate and caring. I hope you will feel good enough about yourselves that you will want to minister to others, and that you will find your own unique ways to do that.